Why We Need to Care for Our Planet

OUR LIFESTYLE

It's important to remember that we are not the only ones living on this planet. It might feel like we are, but we are not. It might seem like social media, shopping centers, or fast food can fulfill our every need, but it can't. We might think all our groceries come from the supermarket and the supermarket alone, but before that, it comes from nature.

Everybody needs to eat and drink. Everybody needs sunshine, fresh air, and clean water.

This is who we are. To get what we need, we have to give something back. If we want to enjoy the gifts of nature, we have to help keep it green.

CONNECTIONS

We use cars and phones, but even without them, we would still survive. Air, water, nutrients, and society are all things we truly can't live without.

To get the most out of life, we need to live healthily — breathing clean air, drinking clean water, and eating quality foods. To be truly healthy, we also need to have people around us.

Everything in nature is interconnected.
We are connected to the planet, and what
we give to it comes back to us.

Because humans and nature
are interconnected, we must remember that
how we treat nature is how nature will treat us.

MODERN LIFE

Jane lived with her parents in a big house. She had the latest smartphone and would buy clothes she rarely wore before tossing them out. She would go to fast-food restaurants, eat from plastic boxes, and drink from plastic cups. Even at home, her fridge was stocked mostly with processed foods, sweets, and junk food from the supermarket, and since she didn't have many friends in real life, she talked to people mostly online, staying up late on her phone.

Jane thought her life was perfect, but one day she woke up, having only slept a few hours, and she didn't want to get out of bed – not even for school. She didn't want to do anything and had completely lost her appetite. Her parents did not know what was wrong, but her body and soul were simply exhausted . . .

A CALL FOR HELP

Earlier, we said that a person needs clean air, sunlight, clean water, quality foods, and sleep. But do we actually get all those things? Because Jane was constantly inundated with too much technology and junk food, her body and soul were desperately crying out for help.

Our planet is asking us for help as desperately as Jane's body is asking her. But can we hear the call? And do we even want to hear it?

LAND CONSERVATION

There's a humble older man named Sir David Attenborough who's been making nature documentaries for a whopping 70 years! He's kind of like a superhero for nature. In his Netflix show, *A Life on Our Planet*, he talks about how he's terribly worried about the Earth because people are doing things that keep hurting nature. But he also shares his hope that things can get better in the future.

When more and more people live on Earth, we use more of its resources. We build bigger cities, grow more crops, and keep more animals for food. All of this takes up space that used to belong to nature. But we need to remember that this land is precious, and we should be careful not to harm it too much by creating too much trash or pollution.

When we use too much of something, it can hurt the plants and animals that live around us. This is called overconsumption, and one of its big problems is that it can make some species disappear forever.

ECOLOGICAL FOOTPRINTS

It's important to remember that both we and the Earth have limits – we can't keep using resources forever without consequences. The Earth is showing us that we're causing harm and we need to pay attention. That's why a system was made to measure how our actions affect the planet.

Ecological footprints help us see how our way of life impacts the Earth by looking at how we use natural resources. When we create things that can break down naturally, it's better for the Earth. But we also need to ask ourselves if we really need to waste water or use electricity in multiple rooms when we're only in one. The Earth gives us what we need, so we should try to use it wisely.

Find out more:

12

THE RAINFOREST

Some of the most amazing things in the world happen in faraway rainforests. It's a place with lots of exotic animals, plants, and trees. Even if we don't live near the rainforest, it still helps us in many ways.

The Amazon is by far the largest rainforest on Earth. The humidity there can reach 100%. The different types of plants are incredible and there is no other place on Earth like it.

The rainforest is nicknamed "the lungs of the planet" not for its high oxygen production, but for its ability to absorb and store carbon dioxide — acting like an air purifier for the entire world.

BIODIVERSITY

When lots of different plants and animals live together in one place, it's called biodiversity. The rainforest is the best example of this. Unfortunately, because of things like farming, mining, and logging, we're losing that biodiversity.

If we compare the biodiversity of the rainforest with a field of palm oil trees, we can see a big difference. The ropes on the palm oil trees are dead, which means it's hard for any plants or animals to live there. Palm oil trees can't do the same important things as the rainforest.

DEFORESTATION

Destroying the rainforest through artificial planting, raising livestock, and building settlements has cost us so much over the past 100 years — we've lost valuable plants and trees, and 50% of animal wildlife. Wild animals now make up only 4% of the earth's mammals.

By cutting down rainforests and their ability to process carbon, greenhouse gases will increase in the atmosphere, leading to more global warming.

Unfortunately, we humans play the biggest role in the destruction of the rainforest.

FARMING

Nature kindly provides for us, but we don't understand the harm we're doing to it by destroying its biodiversity. Wildlife can reproduce naturally, but that's not the case for human systems like farms, fields, and plantations.

The Earth has given us reliable growing conditions for a long time, and we have taken advantage of this. For thousands of years, we humans have been cultivating the land, growing crops, and raising livestock.

It's sad to say, but people weren't happy with what nature gave us. Instead, we became greedy and have been using more and more land to grow food.

OUR SPECIES

Humans are starting to cause a lot of harm to the planet.
The way we use resources and create pollution is stopping the
Earth from being able to heal itself.

We must learn from our mistakes

Nuclear explosions, whether accidental or intentional, are harmful
to all living things. Similarly, we know that cutting down the rainforest
is contributing to the loss of biodiversity.

Less than 100 years ago, there were only 2.3 billion people on earth!

Today, there are 7.9 billion!

In the past, we lived in harmony with nature. We only hunted and ate what we needed, giving the Earth time to replenish its resources and fix our mistakes. But now there are so many of us that the Earth is suffering. This doesn't mean we humans need to disappear, but we must learn to use our resources wisely and regulate our behavior so we don't harm the planet.

It's time to let go of the idea that we're invincible and better than nature. Instead, we need to reconnect with the natural world.

THE MIRACLE OF THE OCEAN

The ocean is the watery part of our planet. It's like the rainforest, only underwater. It helps control the Earth's temperature and humidity, and it can soak up almost all of the planet's carbon dioxide.

Ocean plant life can absorb many more greenhouse gases than the forests on land!

THE CORAL REEF

Did you know that the ocean covers 71% of our planet? Over the past 200 years, the ocean has absorbed a massive 140 billion tons of carbon dioxide! But this has made the water more acidic, which has sadly killed off many types of underwater plants and animals. Global warming has also made the temperature of the ocean rise, which creates more algae than the ocean needs. As a result, half of the ocean's coral reefs have been destroyed. If we don't reduce greenhouse gases, in just 50 years, only a quarter of the reefs will survive.

Another thing that affects the ocean is fishing for too many fish, or "overfishing." Coral reefs use fish excrement for food, so if the fish are removed from the water, the reefs have nothing to eat.

COMMERCIAL FISHING

Overfishing is a bit like taking too many trees from the rainforest.
It can harm the ocean's environment by making it less diverse.
As we have learned, creatures in the ocean rely on each other to live.

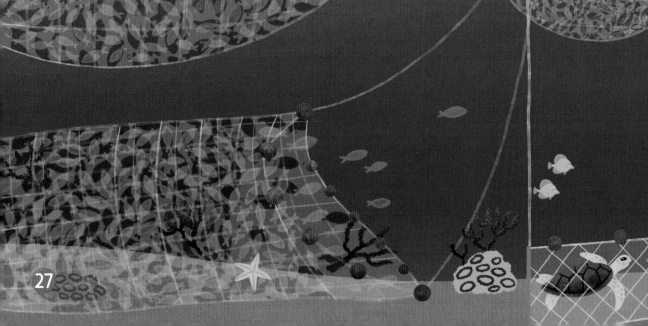

In the past, people used less harmful methods of fishing. This allowed the ocean to recover its fish population. But with the introduction of technology that can locate fish easily, fishing has become more destructive. Fishermen now use trawls, which damage the seabed, causing the loss of 3.9 billion acres of living sea land every year.

As more and more people eat fish, we need to find new ways to harvest them. One way is by growing fish in fish farms. But when fish grow up in a farm, they aren't living in their normal home in the ocean. To grow big and strong, they need extra help, like special foods and medicine. This medicine can end up in the fish we eat, which isn't good for us.

THE OCEAN

Sustainability means using only what we need without taking too much. When it comes to fish, this means only catching what we need to eat. So many fish have been taken from the ocean that it is important to give it time to recover. One way we can help is by rarely eating fish. This will allow the ocean's biodiversity to rejuvenate and we won't have to rely so much on fishing.

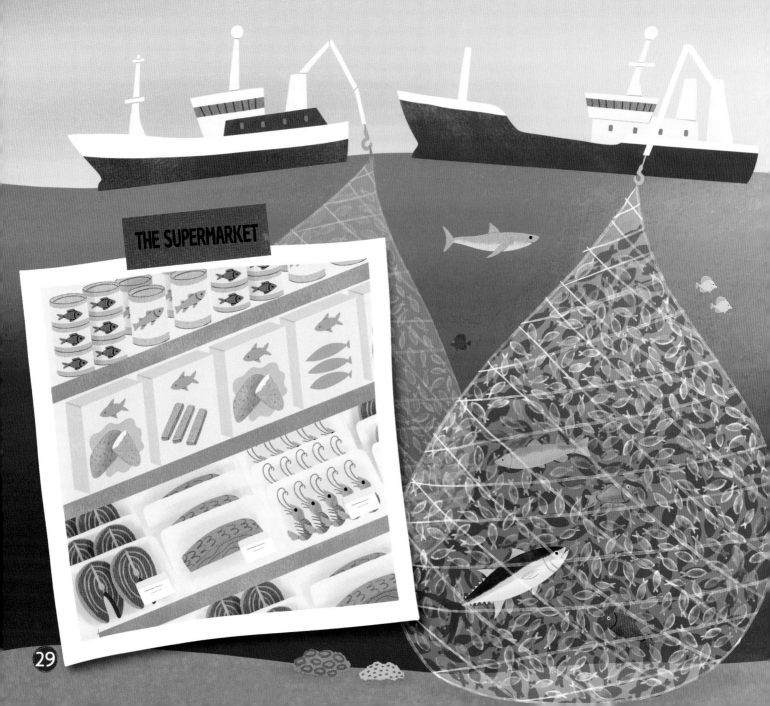

THE SUPERMARKET

People can get official licenses for mass sustainable fishing, but sadly they're not very helpful – many of the world's biggest companies have them, wanting to seem like they're fishing sustainably. But this is not what is truly happening . . .

Big fishing companies catch so many fish that small-scale fishermen can't even catch enough for their own food – making people go hungry in places that already don't have enough food, like the African coast.

LOCAL FISH MARKET

THE EARTH HAS A FEVER

We humans have done so many amazing things since we first started walking the Earth! We've gone all the way to space, explored the deepest parts of the ocean, and even learned how to predict the weather to help us grow crops better.

Nature has always been very helpful to humans, and we've been able to achieve a lot by studying its patterns. But one problem is that as we've made progress, we've also released harmful gases into the air. These gases are making it harder for the planet to cool down naturally, which is causing some big problems.

For 10,000 years, the planet's temperature didn't fluctuate more than 1 degree. But in the last 100 years, global temperatures have risen 1 degree and are quickly approaching 1.5 degrees. It's like when a person has a 1.5-degree temperature increase. When we run a fever, we get sick and have to rest, drink tea, and take vitamins. Similarly – and unfortunately – that is how sick the Earth is right now.

ECOLOGICAL EXTINCTION

As the Earth gets hotter, some gases are building up in the air, making it harder for us to breathe and drink clean water. The rainforests are also getting drier, which means that a fire can start very easily and hurt a lot of animals and plants. This is bad for nature because it's hard for things to grow back to the way they used to be.

BALANCE

Our bodies need balance and stability. This helps our cells (the tiny building blocks that make up our bodies) work the way they should. It also allows us to be happy, have fun, eat good food, and spend time with friends and family.

If we are sick, our bodies become unbalanced and our cells become toxic. It's important to take care of our body, so all of our cells can keep working together to keep us healthy.

This balance is a joint effort between all living things on this planet – humans, plants, and animals. If one of them falls out of the chain, it might be replaced by something else, but if the damage is too great, the chain will eventually die.

BALANCE RESTORED

Remember Jane from earlier? Well, after a while she chose to spend some time in nature – drinking clean water, eating fresh fruits and veggies, staying offline, making real friends, and going on long walks. In a few weeks, she was full of energy and excited to spend more time with her new friends – living proof that we need balance in our lives.

Jane knew she had to change her habits and lifestyle to feel more balanced. She started spending time outside the mall. She had to balance being indoors with being outside with some fresh air and sunshine. Her body is doing much better now that she's drinking water and eating fruits, veggies, and whole grains.

She realized she had to get more sleep and take it easy. When she did, she felt strong, energized, and happy.

Sunshine

Stretch yourself

REST

Go to nature

Slow down

Do you want to know how Jane found balance in her life? Well, she worked hard and took breaks to rest, and in doing so she turned her sadness into joy.

WHAT CAN WE DO FOR YOU, EARTH?

It's hard to say which way is best to help the Earth because scientists have different ideas. But, did you know that the Earth can heal itself? It's like when we take medicine to help our bodies fight sickness. The Earth can regenerate just like our bodies can heal.

The rainforest and the oceans act as our environmental immune system. The key is to restore them to how they were 100 years ago. But how do we bring back their biodiversity?

It's important to eat healthy foods to stay strong and healthy. While it's good to eat meat and fish sometimes, we should try to eat more plants. Did you know that fish get their special Omega-3 fatty acids from eating seaweed? Sometimes, though, fish can have bad things in them like heavy metals and plastics because they help clean up the ocean. So, let's try to eat more fruits, vegetables, and grains, and enjoy fish and meat only in moderation.

YUM! YUM! YUM!

NATURAL 100%

A really cool thing we can do to help the planet is to use a reusable cup when we get drinks. Instead of throwing away plastic cups, we can fill up our special cup with our favorite drink!

Try not to buy too much clothing or any other items that you don't need.

eco

When we eat less meat, we can help the animals and the environment! That's because when we have fewer cows and chickens in the world, there will be more room for other animals to live and grow.

We don't have to become vegetarians, but we should only eat what we need — our great-grandmothers lived to 90 and ate much less meat than we do.

DON'T FORGET: BALANCE IS KEY!

OUR PLANET, OUR LIVES

"No one can do everything, but we can all do something."
—Sylvia Earle, marine biologist and explorer

Why We Need to Care for Our Planet

Parents are highly recommended to watch, and discuss with their children,
the films of Sylvia Earle and David Attenborough,
plus the Netflix documentary *Seaspiracy*, all of which served
as the foundation for this book.

We would also like to thank all natural scientists, authors, and people who
care about this topic and are working to live in harmony with nature.
If you're reading this book, you're one of them!

*In researching this book, we found that expert opinions weren't all the same.
Keep in mind that this isn't a scientific publication, but rather a book that
encourages readers to think critically about the info presented within its pages.
The stories and characters are all fictional.

We strongly encourage you to visit these websites:
https://planetbasedmeals.com
www.footprintcalculator.org

The following websites also helped inform this book:
www.footprintnetwork.org/our-work/ecological-footprint
http://populace.population.city/world
www.greenmatters.com/p/how-overfishing-affects-biodiversity
https://ourworldindata.org/biodiversity-and-wildlife

© Albatros,
an imprint of Albatros Media Group, 2023
5. května 1746/22, Prague 4, Czech Republic
Author: Joli Hannah
Illustrator: Amelia Herbertson
Editor: Scott Alexander Jones

Printed in China by Leo Paper Group.

albatros